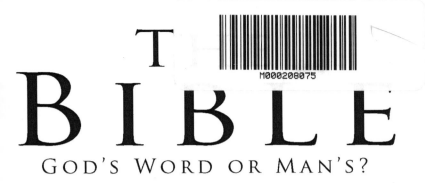

THE BIBLE

GOD'S WORD OR MAN'S?

BRIAN BRODERSEN

Introduction

"For some years now, I have felt uneasy about accepting the whole Bible as the Word of God ... the Holy Bible is an extremely valuable collection of sacred writings. ... But it has weaknesses, and these weaknesses point to why we need an alternative Bible. ... The Bible does not give adequate guidance and teaching on many of today's moral problems."

This statement by a leader in the Church of England demonstrates both the arrogance and the ignorance of so many today concerning the Bible. This statement has no basis whatsoever in reality!

The reality is, the Bible is provably the inspired, inerrant, authoritative, and therefore, eternally relevant Word of God! This is a bold assertion, but in the following pages, I hope to show that it is not simply an idle claim, but an undeniable fact.

Let's begin with a statement from Paul's second epistle to Timothy,

> All Scripture is given by inspiration of God, and is profitable for doctrine, for reproof, for correction, for instruction in righteousness, that the man of God may be complete, thoroughly equipped for every good work.
>
> —2 Timothy 3:16–17

In these two verses, God declares (through Paul) that the Bible is inspired, inerrant, and completely authoritative. First, we will define these terms.

Penned by Man
Inspired by God

Inspired

When we say the Bible is the *inspired* Word of God, what do we mean? We mean that each author was controlled by the Holy Spirit so that the words written weren't his own, but God's. We call this the "verbal inspiration of the Scripture."

However, the writing process was not mechanical. In other words, the Bible wasn't dictated. God did not say to the prophets, "Sit down, get your writing pad out, and record what I say." But rather, God moved miraculously upon chosen men and impressed His thoughts upon them so that they would be writing exactly what God wanted to express to the world.

In all of this, God did not bypass human personality. Jeremiah spoke differently than Isaiah and Ezekiel spoke differently than both of them. They didn't communicate different content, but they did communicate the content distinctly, according to their character. God used a variety of human personalities to express His thoughts.

Peter explains biblical inspiration declaring, "No prophecy of Scripture is of any private interpretation, for [God's Word] never came by the will of man, but holy men of God spoke as they were moved by the Holy Spirit" (2 Peter 1:20). When he says that no prophecy of Scripture is of any private interpretation, he means that the message did not originate with the prophets. They weren't communicating their personal opinions about God. Neither Moses, nor David, nor Zechariah wrote their own ideas about God. Rather, God was moving upon and through these human instruments to communicate what He wanted us to know about Himself.

Inerrancy

Since the Scriptures are inspired, they must also then be *inerrant*, meaning simply "without error." When all the facts are known, the Bible will prove itself to be without error in every matter it addresses, not only spiritual, but also historical, geographical, and scientific. Some people want to relegate the Bible's inerrancy to spiritual matters only. They'll say things like, "The Bible is without error when it deals with matters of faith, but it's full of problems when it comes to anything else." That is completely absurd! Inerrancy means that Scripture does not affirm anything that is contrary to fact.

If the Bible is full of historical, geographical, and scientific mistakes, why would anyone want to believe that it is accurate spiritually? If it isn't right on the lower level of the temporal, material reality, how could we possibly count on the Bible to get eternal issues right?

One of the areas that cause critics to question inerrancy has to do with the absence of "original documents." We do not have the book that Isaiah himself penned or the original copy of Jeremiah's prophecy. We do not have Genesis, Exodus, Leviticus, Numbers, or Deuteronomy, which were penned by Moses. We don't have what Matthew, Luke, John, or Paul penned. Instead, we have copies of what Moses, Jeremiah, and Isaiah wrote. For that reason, the skeptics say, "We can never know for sure what the Bible originally said, nor can we trust the Bible we have today." Well, guess what? We don't have the original document of any piece of classical literature. We only have copies.

So how do we determine if a copy is reliable? How do we know if it really contains what was said in the original document? Well, the more copies that exist, the more they can be compared for consistency, and the greater the case that can be built for a copy being true to the original. The fewer copies that exist, the more difficult it becomes to confirm authenticity; and, the more time that has passed between the copy and the original, the harder it is to know what was originally said.

The ancient writings that are universally accepted and used for historical evidence today—like those of the Greek historian Herodotus, or the Roman historian Tacitus, or even the stories of Homer, who wrote the *Odyssey* and the *Iliad*—are based upon a very small number of manuscripts, and a very long period of time transpired between the original writing and the existing copy.

Among these works, the most manuscript evidence exists for Homer's *Iliad* (six hundred copies), but the time gap between when Homer wrote it and when the copies were made is about twelve hundred years. So we have to trust that in this twelve hundred-year-period, the transcribers got it right, and that what we have is what Homer actually wrote. If you take a college class on ancient Greek literature, most professors will assure you that today's *Iliad* is the same *Iliad* Homer originally

wrote. Now, if scholars are confident that copies based upon
six hundred manuscripts written twelve hundred years after the
author originally penned them are trustworthy, then the writings of the New Testament should not be met with skepticism.
There are over five thousand New Testament manuscripts,
with some of them having less than a one hundred-year gap
between the original documents and the earliest copies!

Authority

Third, the Scriptures are *authoritative*, which means that
the Bible is the final word for faith and practice among indi-
vidual Christians and for the church collectively. However,
the Bible's authority is under attack. Some people say that
the Bible is old-fashioned, outdated, and irrelevant for today.
Jesus Christ didn't see it that way. He said, "For assuredly, I
say to you, till heaven and earth pass away, one jot or one tittle
will by no means pass from the law" (Matthew 5:18).

I am aware that the claim of inspiration is not proof of
inspiration. Other religions claim similar things about their
writings. The big question is, who is right? Is there some over-
riding proof that one is valid and the others are not? Yes, there
is! The Bible not only claims to be the inspired Word of God,
it also includes its own built-in proof. That proof is prophecy.
Prophecy is foretelling the future with one hundred percent
accuracy. We will consider prophecy a bit later, but first let's
look at other types of evidence supporting the biblical claim
to inspiration. Once we see that the Bible is truly inspired, the
fact that it is without error and carries supreme authority must
naturally follow.

SUPPORTING EVIDENCE
FOR INSPIRATION

Indestructibility

First, there is the fascinating fact of the *indestructibility* of the Bible. A very small number of books remain in circulation for one hundred years. The number of books that survive one thousand years is minute.

The Bible, which is over two thousand years old, is not only still in circulation, but is today the world's number one bestseller! When you take into consideration the many attempts throughout history to destroy the Scriptures, its survival is even more amazing!

In AD 303, the Roman Emperor, Diocletian, sought to wipe any trace of Christianity from the face of the earth. He ordered churches to be burned, Christians to be executed, and the Scriptures to be confiscated and destroyed. But Diocletian died, and Christianity kept expanding. Diocletian's successor, Constantine, ordered fifty copies of the Scriptures to be printed at the Roman government's expense! This kind of thing has happened over and over again with the Bible.

Consider this illustration of its indestructibility: Suppose a two thousand-year-old man came walking down the aisle of our church. And suppose we knew that he had been cast into the sea many times, but could not be drowned. He had been thrown to the wild beasts, but was never devoured. He had been made to drink different deadly poisons, but they never did him any harm. He had been bound with strong chains and locked up in prisons and dungeons, but he always managed to shake off the chains and escape. He had been often hung until his enemies thought he was dead, but when they cut him down, he sprang to his feet and walked away again. Hundreds of times they had burnt him at the stake till there seemed to be nothing left of him, but the fires were no sooner out than he leapt from the ashes as well and as strong as before. He had been shot at, stabbed, and cut to pieces, but the pieces came together like little drops of mercury—his wounds healed up at once, and he was none the worse for all this hacking and cutting.

How strange it would seem to look on such a man! Would it not be a great wonder to find him alive and well after all that he had passed through? It would be a wonder indeed. Yet, this is just the way we should feel towards the Bible. This is how the Bible has been treated. It has been burned, drowned, chained, put in prison, buried alive, torn to pieces, and yet it has never been destroyed. It is still the same pure, precious Bible, the same holy, blessed "Book Divine" that it was two thousand years ago.

So the Bible has proven to be indestructible, and its indestructibility, although not proving its divine origin, certainly lends support to the argument.

Historical Veracity

The *historical veracity* of the Bible also supports the Bible being divinely inspired. Over the past two hundred years, the

Bible has been ferociously attacked; but despite the many claims that the Bible is full of historical inaccuracies, to this day, there has never been one proven case.

Critics and skeptics used to think that archaeological investigation and discovery would put the last nail in the coffin of Christianity. But the exact opposite has happened! Archaeology, far from disproving the Bible, has only served to affirm its accuracy.

In 1974, *Time Magazine* published an article, which stated, "After more than two centuries of facing the heaviest scientific guns that could be brought to bear, the Bible has survived, and is perhaps better for the siege. Even on the critic's own terms, historical fact, the scriptures seem more acceptable now than when the rationalists began the attack."

That's a bold admission. They're admitting that for two hundred years, critics have been trying to disprove the Bible, but have utterly failed.

The following examples represent some of the critics' failed attempts to disprove the historical accuracy of the Bible:

Critics argued against Moses' authorship of the first five books of the Bible. They claimed that Moses couldn't have written those books because there was no written language during his time. As has always been the case, the critics were wrong! Not only was there writing at the time of Moses, archeologists discovered libraries from before the time of Abraham, who, incidentally, lived four hundred years before Moses. One such discovery was made in Abraham's birthplace,

Ur of the Chaldees, a city still existing in modern day Iraq. This archeological find completely disproved the claims that there had been no writing at the time of Moses.

Because there was no record of a Hittite Empire apart from the Bible, critics argued for years that biblical references to the nation of the Hittites were pure myth. Again, archaeologists discovered that the Hittites existed, and that they had possessed a vast empire covering the region now known as Turkey. So again, through archaeological discoveries, the Bible was found to be absolutely accurate.

Critics also argued that Pontius Pilate never existed in history because the only record of his life was found in the New Testament. Well, guess what happened? Archaeologists were digging in the area of Caesarea on the coast of Israel when they found a stone engraved with the name of Pontius Pilate. It stated that he was the governor of Judea at the exact period of time the New Testament claims!

From the mid-1700s through the mid-1900s, archaeology has systematically disproved everything the critics have ever put forth as an argument against the historical veracity of the Scriptures. You can trust the historical accuracy of the Bible.

Scientific Accuracy

The *scientific accuracy* of the Bible is another area that reinforces rather than casts doubt on the Bible being inspired. How many times has it been said, "The Bible is full of scientific errors," or "The Bible and science contradict each other"? This is simply not true. The burden of proof is on those who make the claim. There are no scientific errors in Scripture. Some say, "What about evolution?" Well, is evolution provable? We can prove that the Bible is the Word of God much easier than evolutionists can prove their theory.

The Bible is not a book of science, yet no scientific observation in the Bible contradicts known scientific evidence. Every other religion's literature contains certain unscientific views of astronomy, medicine, hygiene, etc. The Bible is absolutely free from the scientific absurdities so common among sacred or religious texts. As a matter of fact, thirty-five hundred years ago, Moses said, "The life of the flesh is in the blood" (Leviticus 17:11). His declaration was confirmed by scientists in the seventeenth century. Three thousand years ago, David said, "The sun is moving in a circuit through the heavens" (see Psalm 19:5–6). It wasn't that long ago when people were saying that the Bible must certainly be mistaken because everyone knows the sun doesn't move. Now we know that the sun is moving! Two thousand years ago, Paul the apostle spoke of creation being in the bondage of decay (Romans 8:21–22). This scientific fact was documented in 1850 and from then on referred to as the Second Law of Thermodynamics.

Far from promoting superstition and scientific error, the Bible makes statements that are in complete harmony with what is today common knowledge.

One more example of the Bible's scientific accuracy can be found in Genesis 15. In this chapter, God implied to Abraham that the stars were innumerable, whereas up until the seventeenth century, it was thought that the stars numbered in the thousands. Today astronomers acknowledge the truth of what God had said so long ago in His Word—the stars are innumerable.

Harmony of the Scriptures

The *harmony of the Bible* is truly amazing. It was written by at least forty different authors, composed over a fifteen hundred to four thousand-year period of time, and written on three different continents in three different languages. Yet, the Bible is still one book. It has one doctrinal system, one moral standard, and one plan of salvation. In this regard, the Bible is unparalleled in history.

Can you imagine, from a human standpoint, that anything like this could have ever happened? Forty different authors—disconnected from one another by time and space—spoke on the most controversial matters known to mankind and yet came up with an absolutely harmonious record of all of these things. It's nothing less than a miracle. That simply couldn't happen, humanly speaking. The harmony of the Bible is yet another support to the Bible's claim to be of divine origin.

All of the aforementioned—the harmony of the Bible, the scientific accuracy, the historical veracity, and the indestructibility—lend support to the claim of biblical inspiration, inerrancy, and authority, but they don't prove it. I think they come awfully close, but the biblical proof of its claim to be the Word of God is, as already stated, found in predictive prophecy.

PROPHECY—THE BUILT-IN PROOF OF THE BIBLE'S INSPIRATION

Predictive prophecy is the built-in proof that the Bible is the Word of God. In Isaiah 46:9–10, God said, "For I am God, and there is no other; I am God, and there is none like Me, declaring the end from the beginning, and from ancient times things that are not yet done." To truly predict the future is an ability that God alone possesses.

Prophecy is not pronouncing vague, generalized predictions, but giving specific details of things before they happen. This is exactly what we find in the Bible.

Prophecy Concerning the Jewish People

In approximately AD 32, Jesus spoke of the future of Jerusalem and the Jewish people.

> "When you see Jerusalem surrounded by armies, then know that its desolation is near. … For these are the days of vengeance, that all things that are written may be fulfilled. … For there will be great distress in the land and wrath upon this people. And they will fall by the edge of the sword, and be led captive into all nations. And Jerusalem will be trampled by Gentiles until the times of the Gentiles are fulfilled."
>
> —Luke 21:20–24

Just as Jesus predicted, in AD 70, the Roman general Titus destroyed Jerusalem, slaughtered a million Jews, and led over one hundred thousand Jews away into captivity. For nearly two thousand years, the Jews were dispersed among the nations and Jerusalem was overrun by one foreign power after another. It wasn't until 1948 that the Jews finally returned to their homeland.

Prophecies Concerning the Messiah

Jesus fulfilled hundreds of Messianic prophecies. Here are just a few examples:

Seven hundred years before the birth of Christ, Micah wrote:

> But you Bethlehem Ephrathah, though you are little among the thousands of Judah, yet out of you shall come forth to Me the One to be Ruler in Israel, whose goings forth are from old, from everlasting.

—Micah 5:2

Luke records the fulfillment:

> And it came to pass in those days that a decree went out from Caesar Augustus that all the world should be registered. ... So all went to be registered, everyone to his own city. Joseph also went up from Galilee, out of the city of Nazareth, into Judea, to the city of David, which is called Bethlehem, because he was of the house and lineage of David, to be registered

with Mary, his betrothed wife, who was with child. So it was, that while they were there, the days were completed for her to be delivered. And she brought forth her firstborn Son, and wrapped Him in swaddling cloths, and laid Him in a manger.

—Luke 2:1–7

Five hundred years before the time of Christ, Zechariah wrote:

Rejoice greatly, O daughter of Zion! Shout, O daughter of Jerusalem! Behold, your King is coming to you; He is just and having salvation, lowly and riding on a donkey. A colt, the foal of a donkey.

—Zechariah 9:9

Matthew records the fulfillment:

Now when they drew near Jerusalem, and … the Mount of Olives, Jesus sent two disciples, saying to them, "Go into the village opposite you, and immediately you will find a donkey tied, and a colt with her. Loose them and bring them to Me." … All this was done that it might be fulfilled which was spoken by the prophet, saying: "Tell the daughter of Zion, 'Behold, your King is coming to you, lowly, and sitting on a donkey, a colt, the foal of a donkey.'" So the disciples went and did as Jesus commanded them. They brought the donkey and the colt, laid their clothes on them, and set Him on them. And a very great multitude spread their clothes on the road; others cut down branches from the trees and spread them on the road. Then the multitudes who went before and those who followed cried out, saying: "Hosanna [save now] to the Son of David! 'Blessed is He who comes in the name of the LORD!' Hosanna [save now] in the highest!"

—Matthew 21:1–9

Lastly, one thousand years before the time of Christ, David wrote:

They pierced My hands and My feet; I can count all My bones. They look and stare at Me. They divide My garments among them, and for My clothing they cast lots.

—Psalm 22:16–18

Mark records the fulfillment:

And they brought Him to the place Golgotha, which is translated, Place of a Skull. Then they gave Him wine mingled with myrrh to drink, but He did not take it. And when they crucified Him [hands and feet pierced], they divided His garments, casting lots for them to determine what every man should take.

—Mark 15:22–24

These are just a small sampling of the prophecies fulfilled by Jesus Christ. It is a mathematical impossibility that Jesus of Nazareth could have fulfilled all the prophecies He did and not be the promised Messiah.

Prophecy Concerning the End Times

Prophecies concerning the end times and the second coming of Christ also need to be mentioned. Without going into detail, these prophecies concern the restoration of the Jewish people to their homeland, Jerusalem as the center of world conflict, the resurrection of the Roman Empire, a one-world economy, a one-world religion, and the rise of a world dictator. You don't have to look far to see how the stage is being set for the fulfillment of these prophecies. The nation of Israel is back in the Promised Land. Jerusalem has become a burden to the surrounding nations. The European Union has united Europe in a way that has not been experienced since the days of the Roman Empire. Globalization is the goal of many world leaders, as seen in the activity and declarations of the United Nations. Now, all that's needed is someone to unite all men together. That someone is coming to be sure. He is called Antichrist!

All of these things give proof that the Bible is the work of someone outside our space-time continuum, someone who sees the end from the beginning. That someone is of course God!

You can trust the Bible. You can trust it for what it says about history, science, and geography. You can trust it for what it says about man, his origin, and his purpose. You can trust what it says about God, who He is, what He's done, and what He's going to do; and you can trust it for what it says about the eternal destiny of those who believe in Christ and those who don't! You can trust it from Genesis to Revelation. You can trust it more than you can trust the sun rising tomorrow. Remember what Jesus said, "Heaven and earth will pass away, but My words will by no means pass away" (Matthew 24:35).

Recommended Reading

From God to Us
Norman Geisler and William Nix

How We Got the Bible
Neil Lightfoot

The Books and the Parchments
F. F. Bruce

The Canon of Scripture
F. F. Bruce

The New Testament Documents: Are They Reliable?
F. F. Bruce

The Origin of the Bible
Philip Wesley Comfort

The Word of Truth
R. Sheehan

Contact Information

If you have questions or would like to pray with someone, please call the following numbers:

In the US:
714 979 4422

In the UK:
+44 (0)20 8466 5365

You may also go to the following website for more information:

www.backtobasicsradio.com